THE MODERN

A TOURIST'S GUIDE TO THE
BRITISH

by Simon Henry

Illustrations by Mark Bennington

Nightingale

An imprint of Wimbledon Publishing Company
LONDON

Copyright © 2000
Illustrations © 2000 WPC

First published in Great Britain in 2000
by Wimbledon Publishing Company Ltd
P.O. Box 9779 London SW19 7ZG
All rights reserved

First published 2000 in Great Britain

ISBN: 1903222 06 0

Produced in Great Britain
Printed and bound in Hungary

This book aims to illuminate some of the dark recesses of a confusing and often confused people - the British. Given Britain's modest size, its inhabitants display remarkable differences: each region boasting its own particular quirks and foibles, strange mannerisms and silly accent.

Ranging fearlessly from North to South, I have attempted to be as fair and even-handed as possible - subjecting each region to the same rigorous, meticulous and objective standards of sociological investigation. That said, my comments and conclusions ought to be taken with a liberal pinch of salt (and a dash of malt vinegar, according to taste).

This is a book for tourist and resident alike. The British have a long tradition of self-ridicule and hopefully the following pages will provide some humorous home truths.

For tourists, I hope this book will be a souvenir of their stay, and that it will prove to be a little more substantial than the scale model of Buckingham Palace, or tartan dish cloths which are often rashly purchased.

SIMON HENRY
1999

ESSEX

The people of Essex are noted for two things: their considerable wealth, whether hard earned (from skilled manual jobs), or stolen (from banks); and their propensity to spend this wealth on tasteless living. Essex men can be found in futuristic wine bars, posing in designer suits and sunglasses. Here, they drink 'iced' lagers from the bottle and discuss the merits of different night-clubs, with names like Ritzy and Samantha's. Meanwhile, the girls of the county are particularly fêted for their ability to conduct scores of casual physical relationships, and their disinclination to wear undergarments (thus facilitating these relationships). Unsurprisingly, the repressed majority of the British public views the ambitious and fun-loving Essex population with considerable jealousy.

WEST MIDLANDS

The West Midlands is centred on Britain's second largest city, Birmingham, which is inhabited by the Brummie. Emerging as a bold challenge to London's economic dominance, Birmingham has been seen to flout tradition and heritage even down to the nuances of the English accent. Whereas many Londoners revere the Queen's English and pay close attention to pronunciation, the Brummie employs a bunged-up, dreary whine to cock a snook at the language. Furthermore, rebellious instincts have fuelled Birmingham's current prosperity. The city has realised that the smart money today is not, as Londoner's would believe, in banking, it's in curry. With several hundred Balti Houses on most streets in the Midlands, Birmingham boasts more small businesses per square metre than any other region of the country.

MANCHESTER

The Mancunian is an expert in two vital areas of human endeavour: dancing and football. The city's night life and music scene are legendary and the football team is the most famous in the world. Your chances of spotting a Mancunian who finds difficulty in performing complicated dance manoeuvres are as slim as Manchester United suffering a defeat. Mother Nature attempts to dampen the Mancunian's innate *joie de vivre* with a practical meteorological joke - rain, rain and more rain. However, since the invention of indoor night-clubs, covered stadia and ecstasy, the Mancunian has sported a permanent grin.

CUMBRIA

The Cumbrian is at his happiest when kitted out in a brightly-coloured fleece, khaki shorts and a pair of stout walking boots. Inside his rucksack nestle a Thermos flask, full of sweet tea, and a Tupperware plastic box, containing 'potted meat' sandwiches. Climbing a large, steep hill on a dark winter's day, legs exposed to the elements, is clearly not everyone's idea of fun. Still less is the prospect of sitting down at the summit to consume a sweet tea and potted meat sandwich picnic. However, dedication to this exhausting and seemingly ridiculous activity produces beneficial medical effects. Despite the onset of visible varicose veins and liver spots, Cumbrian pensioners effortlessly trot up the one-in-four gradients without even stopping to catch their breath.

THE POTTERIES

After a hard day at the kiln-face, the potter is faced with a difficult choice. Does he eat his beloved chips, or does he opt for the more traditional delicacy of the oatcake (a flat, savoury form of nutrition)? Most of the time he will go for both. This love of food stems from the essential trade of the area. With infamous companies, such as Royal Doulton and Wedgwood located in the vicinity, manufacturing plates and dishes, not to mention tureens and sundry other food-based receptacles, the temptation to eat from them proves too much for the potter. This self-contained universe, this island of proud and skilled craftsmanship, is therefore populated by exceptionally dextrous gluttons.

THE HOME COUNTIES

Inhabitants of these counties on London's picturesque fringes regard neatness as the highest virtue. Shrubs and privets neatly delineate the boundaries of their well-preserved gardens and while they are not commuting to and from their London offices, or sitting at their desks, they can be found tending to the lawn - ensuring that their grass is more perfectly clipped than next door's. In this pleasantly competitive world of 'Keeping up with the Joneses', net curtains are *de rigeur*, the employment of a part-time cleaner a prerequisite and buffing of the family saloon with turtle wax on a Sunday morning is considered to be absolutely vital.

YORKSHIRE

The county is famed for its Yorkshire pudding, which, contrary to first impressions, is not a dessert delicacy, but rather a stodgy and tasteless main course accompaniment, consisting of flour, milk and eggs. Dependence upon this doughy (and cheap) staple suits Yorkshire's dour and skinflint inhabitants down to their (second-hand) bootstraps. They are people of few words - and the few words they do use are 'no', 'can't', 'won't' and similarly negative monosyllables. Yorkshire folk will occasionally smile - usually when they are about to pass wind - but more generally view optimism and enjoyment as luxuries they can ill afford.

THE WEST COUNTRY

Excessive consumption of a noxious and highly intoxicating home-brewed cider, 'scrumpy', is the West Country inhabitant's weakness. While some weaknesses - an inability to speak fluent Portuguese, for example - do not pose undue health risks, addiction to scrumpy most certainly does. The typical resident's face is permanently reddened from the brew's effects and the slow, slurred delivery of the West Country drawl is blamed on its addling qualities. Even before drinking scrumpy, the West Country yokel is a relaxed and thoroughly contented soul. Following its consumption, the yokel is literally horizontal.

EAST ANGLIA

Sandringham, the Queen's English estate, is located here with the direct result that the East Anglian hankers after the life of the aristocratic country farmer. Unfortunately, a bizarre tendency to pronounce the word 'beautiful' as 'boooootiful' whenever an oven-ready turkey - a delicacy of the region - appears on his dining table, betrays his non-aristocratic credentials. (The Queen and the aristocracy never eat oven-ready turkeys and they always pronounce every word perfectly in the Queen's English.) These class-based *faux pas* do not arrest the East Anglian's aristocratic pretensions; the wearing of a waxed jacket and the use of a walking stick (whether or not he has a limp) are sure signs of his social-climbing tendencies.

LONDON
(WEST END)

The West End of London is populated by the most fashionable, *chic* and generally hip indviduals in Britain. Whether discussing the music business in a famous celebrity bar, dating models, shopping in designer boutiques or scowling at the tourists, these trendies tend to exude an air of confident superiority. Residing cheek-by-jowl with these prosperous and *avant-garde* are the practitioners of the vice trade: strippers, sex shop proprietors and prostitutes. This underworld guarantees disorientation for the first time tourist who, moments after spotting Hugh Grant in a small sushi restaurant, is offered 'dope-hash-heroine-girls-crack-speed-sex' by shifty passers-by.

LONDON
(EAST END)

The East End of London is populated by salt-of-the-earth entrepreneurs who spend their days shouting at passers-by from their market stalls. 'Three melons for a pound', or 'Half-price yashmaks' are common catch-phrases of the East End stall holder. Unlike his West End counterparts, the Eastender says what he means and means what he says. Although the goods on the stalls may well be 'hot', the melons will indeed retail at three for a pound and the yashmaks will be of fantastic quality. Luckily, the East End's reputation for harbouring gangsters means that local police are usually far too busy coping with organised crime to bother hassling the small fry in Stepney market who sell Gucci watches at £20 a time.

LONDON
(CITY)

The City of London provides the bulk of Britain's earnings, now that the factories and mills have been closed. The relatively few people in Britain who work in the City are therefore exceedingly rich. Ask an ambitious City of London worker how much he/she earns and the reply will come, 'Not enough.' This equates to approximately one million pounds per year, before bonus payments, share options and perks. The City type works on average between seventeen and twenty-one hours per day, and when he/she is away from the trading desk is easily spotted: passed out on a wine bar table and surrounded by several bottles of Dom Perignon rosé.

The Glaswegian is less likely than other Scots to don the traditional costume of the kilt - preferring instead to spend his hard-earned social security money on McEwans Export and unfiltered cigarettes. The former accounts for the high brawl-per-pub ratio in the city, the latter for the unparalleled rate of cardiac arrest. When his money manages to stretch to other essentials, such as food, he may well indulge in a battered Mars bar - just to ensure that his heart is offered no respite. The Glaswegian is thought to hold unshakeable and well-reasoned opinions relating to this suicidal lifestyle, but the delivery of his dialect is so coarse and fast-paced that he is rendered entirely unintelligible.

KENT

The Garden of England, where hops and apples are harvested every summer-time by this simple, agricultural people, is also blessed with Britain's closest coast to France. Cigarettes and alcohol are half-price over the Channel, so the not-*so*-simple Kentish residents disappear for days on end, returning from their trips with lorry-loads of cheap luxuries which they sell at a considerable profit. With such a plentiful supply of cut-price tobacco and booze, the Kentish smuggler is subjected to constant temptation and thoroughly enjoys indulging in the simple pleasures afforded by this influx of intoxicants. Many argue, however, that no profit can really make up for having to spend so much time in Calais.

SOUTH WALES

The people of South Wales are not keen Welsh speakers. Indeed, they are not keen speakers at all, preferring instead to communicate by singing. Shirley Bassey and Tom Jones are leading exponents of the craft, but even the humblest former miner can recite operatic arias at will. During their frequent sing-songs, South Welsh eyes become moist, and tears of joy and pride stream down their faces, as their perfectly-pitched harmonies fill the air. This apparently childish display of emotion is explained in part by the endearing South Welsh tradition of calling everyone 'boyo'.

SOUTH COAST RESORTS

When old elephants feel their time is near, they traipse off alone into the sunset. When the elderly southern English middle-classes acquire that same sixth sense, they sell their homes and migrate to south coast sea resorts, such as Eastbourne and Bournemouth. Traditionally, men die earlier than women, so these resorts are populated by widows in see-through plastic headscarves, unfashionable, nylon dresses and support tights, who amble along the promenade with the aid of zimmer frames or walking sticks. The south coast widows provide excellent custom for the cafés (particularly those serving cut-price cream teas) but they do not provide ideal sunbathing specimens for the eager naturist photographer.

THE NORTH EAST

The Geordie lives in the cool, intemperate climate of Newcastle in the north-east of England. Excessive intake of suet (particularly in meat pies) is therefore considered essential, providing layers of insulation via the trusted media of fat and cellulite. Geordies of both sexes are fanatical supporters of their football team and, as a result of their insulation, are able to attend the games - even in the deepest winter - wearing only a thin replica shirt, without even the inkling of a shiver. Following the football, Geordies stand outside public houses, drinking brown ale, chanting the phrase 'Howay the lads' and patting their oversized stomachs with considerable pride.

OXFORD & CAMBRIDGE

The twin ancient university cities are idyllic centres of learning, culture and architectural majesty, spoiled only by the students resident there. By day, the pretentious undergraduates in distinctive college scarves ride their bicycles along the cobbled streets, reciting epic Greek poetry or complicated mathematical formulae to their peers. By night, they stage humorous reviews or obscure plays and buy vintage champagnes or port on Daddy's credit card. Following final examinations, taken in full evening dress, the students are doused with flour, double cream and confetti by their friends - in a ritual as arcane as the universities themselves. Dry cleaners in the ancient university cities are particularly busy in June.

Wales has its own language, Welsh, a specialised tongue practised predominantly in the north of the country. Llanfairpwllgwngyllgorgerychwynorgerychwyrndrobwllllantysiliogogogoch - the name of a northern town - illustrates why those in the south prefer the simpler (and shorter) English language. Welsh words are formed in the back of the throat before the speaker literally spits them out. Northern Welsh-speakers are rightly proud of their linguistic abilities and positively revel in the spray which accompanies their native conversations. The Welsh Prince, Charles, has learned to speak the language, but he rarely uses it - especially in the company of his mother, the Queen, who is known to detest spitting.

SCOTLAND

Which other people in the world have a highly alcoholic drink, Scotch, named after them? As well as heavy bouts of drinking, the inhabitants of Scotland are characterised by their penchant for cross-dressing, a practice often attributed to the effects of heavy drinking. The men wear skirts, known as kilts, and the women often wear trousers, known as trousers. To retain their masculinity, however, Scottish men do not wear undergarments beneath their kilts - even during Scotland's severe winter months. An inevitable result of this habit is that the Scottish male suffers from the droopiest scrota in the western world, as well as painful frostbite. The tendency of the Scot to scowl and moan is often attributed to these unfortunate medical conditions.

LONDON
(COCKNEY)

The cockney is a Londoner, born within ear shot of the Bow Bells, whose linguistic and sartorial mores are a mystery to non-cockneys. A suit bedecked with pearls provides the traditional cockney costume, though the popularity of the pearly attire has waned since modern textiles such as acrylic were invented. Still, the cockney's rhyming slang remains a popular form of communication. If a cockney says: 'That's an Ayrton, my old China', he means you owe him ten pounds - and that he considers you a friend. (Translation: Ayrton = Ayrton Senna = Tenner = Ten pounds. 'Senna' and 'Tenner' rhyme. China = China Plate = Mate. 'Plate' and 'Mate' rhyme.) Given his cheery, chirpy and cheeky demeanour, only the hardest souls would not willingly pay up.

LIVERPOOL

A resident of the city is called a scouser - named after a sailor's dish of stewed meat with vegetables and ship's biscuits (Lobscouse), illustrating Liverpool's historic affinity with the sea. It is said that sailors used to sing about their ghastly meals when they returned to dock and The Beatles were inspired by this sea-faring tradition with songs such as 'Yellow Submarine'. Liverpool's musical tradition is underpinned by the scouser's method of speech which modulates in an almost operatic manner - leaving the listener feeling faintly seasick.

LANCASHIRE

During the nineteenth century, the county's cotton trade dominated the planet. Since losing this industry to developing nations, Lancastrians have instead become world leaders in the less profitable practice of gurning. Gurning is a method of contorting the face to ludicrous and horrifying lengths - an activity facilitated by the removal of the gurner's dentures. Some experts argue that gurning began when Lancashire women began to wear itchy polyester lingerie instead of the more comfortable and traditional cotton gussets. Still, Lancashire's women have proved their ability to accept a miserable lot and come out gurning.

NOTTINGHAM

The city was the scene of several bloody fifteenth century battles between Robin Hood and the wicked Sheriff. It is said the carnage inflicted on the male population is still in evidence today. The male inhabitants are heavily outnumbered by the city's womenfolk: with the predictable result that the smile on the typical Nottingham male's face rivals that of the self-satisfied Cheshire cat. In a desperate attempt to attract the few men, the descendants of Maid Marion beautify themselves to an extent unseen in the remainder of the British Isles, making the cosmetics counter of the Nottingham-based chemist, Boots, the busiest in the country.

CORNWALL

As the southernmost point of the mainland, Cornwall stands between Britain and the foreigner. But speaking in a mystifying English dialect (Cornish), and providing the rest of the British population with enticing holiday destinations, means the Cornish are almost foreigners in their own country. The sight of Cornish youths surfing the unusually large waves with the panache of American Pacific coast dudes, combined with the startling Cornish predilection for 'keeping it in the family', only adds to this sense of difference. However, Cornwall's British credentials are restored by gastronomy, as the famous Cornish Pasty was invented here.

NEW TOWNS

New towns, like Milton Keynes and Welwyn Garden City are inhabited by white collar workers, noted for the pristine condition of their white collars. The resident's fastidious attention to his collars is explained by the fact that there is little to do (outside office hours) in new towns except to ensure that one's white collars are in perfect condition for one's white collar work. New towns have no sense of history, no sporting traditions and no community spirit, so the conversation of the typical resident is entirely devoted to the whiteness of his collars and the white collar nature of his occupation.

NORTHERN SEASIDE RESORTS

In times past, the British decamped en masse to resorts such as Blackpool during the summer months, attracted by the comforting sound of lapping waves and the beauty of the unspoiled sands. Victorian ladies under elegant parasols delighted in taking a relaxing stroll along the promenade, ensuring, of course that their ankles were always fully covered. Children shrieked with glee as they rode the donkeys on the beach, while the Victorian male would don his stripey bathing suit before conducting a robust breast stroke in the icy waters. Now, as the sea and beaches have suffered the indignity of increasing pollution, the formerly civilised standards of conduct have plummeted. The contemporary resort, a mecca of down-at-heel pubs, noisy amusement arcades and casinos is populated by gangs of restless juveniles and gambling addicts, whose ghastly manners would have reduced the prim Victorian ladies to tears.

OLDE ENGLISH
TOWNS

Britain has existed for many centuries, and pockets of its history have remained virtually untouched by the modern age. The resident of the olde English town is a testament to this phenomenon. In Stratford-upon-Avon, birthplace of William Shakespeare, even the least educated resident naturally speaks the Bard's Elizabethan blank verse at will. The citizenry of Bath are thoroughly au fait with the history of Roman Britain and the Latin language provides a useful tool of verbal communication. Meanwhile, Windsor's lengthy association with the throne is underpinned by the convention that all townsfolk are able to recite at least seven centuries worth of royal genealogy...At least this is what the travel guides would have you believe - all an intriguing fiction of course, and one that ironically ensures that all these places are almost entirely populated by tourists for most of the year.